VEI

GREECE

<u>WITHOUT   TEARS</u>

A HOW-TO, HOW-NOT-TO,
WHERE-TO,WHERE-NOT-TO
WHAT-TO, WHAT-NOT-TO
VISITORS' GUIDE
AND
SURVIVAL COURSE

*Title plagiarized and paraphrased from Marc Van Doren's **<u>Shakespeare without tears.</u>** Forgive me.

ISBN 960 226 430 6

Distributed by
EFSTATHIADIS GROUP S.A.
HEAD OFFICE: AGIOU ATHANASIOU ST. GR - 145 65 ANIXI ATTIKIS
TEL: (01) 8140602, 8140702 FAX: (01) 8142915 TELEX: 216176 EF
ATHENS BRANCH: 14 VALTETSIOU ST. GR - 106 80 ATHENS
TEL: (01) 3633319, 3614312, 3637284 FAX: (01) 3614312
ATHENS BOOKSHOP: 84 ACADEMIAS ST. TEL: 3637439
THESSALONIKI BRANCH: 4 C. CRISTALLI ST. ANTIGONIDON SQUARE
THESSALONIKI, GR - 546 30 TEL: (031) 511781, 542498, FAX 544759
THESSALONIKI BOOKSHOP: 14 ETHNIKIS AMINIS ST. TEL: (031) 278158

Printed and bound in Greece by
EFSTATHIADIS GROUP S.A.

Athens 1993

Written by	**Vernon Vas Elliott**
Illustrated by	**Vernon Vas Elliott**
Copyright by	**Vernon Vas Elliott**
Edited by	**Vernon Vas Elliott**
Statistics by	**Vernon Vas Elliott**

To all those who,
having visited Greece,
still love her.

And to my other two sons, Bill and Gregg,
who love Greece after many visits.

And to their mother, Sharon,
who set me free to fly my kites.

And to Natashita
without whose help and encouragement,
not to mention expertise in this damned machine,
nothing was possible.

But most of all to Greece itself,
a constant source of inspiration,
and to the Greeks,
a constant source of frustration,
and sometimes joy.

3

PAXOS or PAXI

SYROS or SYRA

4

DISCLAIMER(S)

The information contained within is as reliable as anything could possibly be in this wondrous land and it is subject to change without any prior notice or even a memo. For that matter, it may have changed several times already.

Also, because few of us (Greeks I mean) are hampered by such inadequacies as attention to details, please overlook the occasional and sometimes frequent misplacement of commas, misspelled words etc.

If you are reading this before deciding on a trip to Greece, there is a reasonably unreliable pre-test which could give you some clues and-or hints as to how much or how little you'll enjoy your trip. Then again, maybe it won't.

If you are already there, or here (in Greece I mean) OH WELL, read the book, cross your fingers, dial-a-prayer and ΚΑΛΗ ΤΥΧΗ - KALEE TEEHEE - GOOD LUCK!!!!!

In Greece you find something
more
than any other place on earth,
you find yourself.

Lawrence   Durrell

CONTENTS

I

READING GREEK
(a real short-cut)

φ σ ε=Φ Σ E

Reading Greek is not nearly as ominous a task as it may appear at first. Here, reference must be made to GREEK: A FRACTURED LEXICON, unquestionably the most graphic and least authoritative work on the Greek alphabet and its pronunciation since the Phoenicians.

Briefly and encouragingly, there are only 24 letters in the Greek alphabet, 14 of which are immediately recognisable. Four of this group unfortunately have an altogether different pronunciation than they do in English for reasons entirely unclear to me.

To begin with, let's take those which we recognise as well as those which have similar sounds:

A-α-a flat as in CAR

E-ε-e always as in GET, LET, NET

Z-z- as in ZOO, ZIP, ZAP

I-ι- ee as in PIECE

M-μ-m as in MAMA

O-o-o as in DOG, MOB, SOB

T-τ as in TOP, TIP, TAP

N-v-n as in NOT, NOW, NIL

Now there are those we recognise on one hand, but for some whimsical reason have a different sound:

B-β-b is actually a V as in VICTOR

H-η is really like a Greek I- ee as in PIECE

P-ρ is the same as R-r only rrrrolled

Y-y is also like an I- ee as in PIECE

X-x not like in EXXON but a harsh h as in ha-ha-ha-ha

IN THE FIRST CATEGORY THERE IS ALSO

K-κ- k as in KING
which we forgot, but there is enough room here , thank goodness.

Now we have those we do not recognise on sight but whose sounds are virtually familiar:

Δ-δ   TH as in THEM

Θ-θ   TH as in THINK

Λ-λ   L as in LIE, LAY, LAUGH

Π-π   P as in PIE, POP, TOP

Σ-σ   S as in SISTER

Φ-φ   F as in FEAR

Ω-ω   O same as the O in TOP, POT, LOT

And finally those we recognise neither by sight nor by sound. Be brave, don't give up, there are only three of them.

Γ-γ   as in YES, YEA, YONDER
       In desperation try a very soft G.

Ξ-ξ   KS or X in LAX, TAX, FAX

Ψ-ψ   PS as in LAPSE, COLLAPSE, ELAPSE

I have been referring to the CAPITAL letters only. The small ones, provided for you directly next to the capitals, are another story. But why complicate matters I always say.

That's all. It wasn't that bad after all.

OK. Now there are a variety of letter combinations that make some rather unique sounds but for the sake of brevity, if not academic achievement, we shall dispense with them for the time being and maybe forever.

Oftentimes many of the store signs are in English or Greenglish, a strange yet colorful language which unfortunately is disappearing as the level of English language instruction is improving. Many street signs, highway signs etc. are in latin as well as in Greek characters. A sampling of a few is provided both for your information and amusement.

So we find RESTORANTS, BAGERIS, MEALES

MOTORBEIKES TO RENT, CITY GENTERS, BEAUTY

SALOONS, SPAGETI, and WINNING KILOMETERS!!!!!

14

Then we have English words but alas written in Greek for your ..... convenience as well as the snobbery of those who may know some English but want you to think that they know a lot more.

To be able to read those signs a few more details are necessary.

In Greek, there are no letters to make the sounds of B, D, G, so the Greeks, creative and inventing souls that they are, put together letter combinations to make up the deficiency.

B = MP   D = NT   G = Γ K or TZ as in parking
                                        or in George

but there is none for SH so inevitably SHED becomes SED, and SHIP turns to SIP.

A few modest examples are next, both for your enlightment and practice.

5 of 20 is excellent
4 of 20 is good to average
3 of 20 is poor
2 - 1 - 0 YOU FAIL. YOU MUST BUY
                    GREEK: A FRACTURED LEXICON

First we will test you on English words spelled in Greek:

1. ΡΕΣΤΟΡΑΝ ....

2. ΜΠΑΡ ....

3. ΦΙΛΜ ....

4. ΠΑΡΤΥ ....

5. ΣΕΞΥ ....

6. ΣΤΟΠ ....

7. ΣΤΡΕΣΣ ....

8. ΡΗΛΑΞ ....

9. ΚΑΜΠΙΝΓΚ ....

10. ΦΑΣΤΦΟΥΝΤ(ΑΔΙΚΟ) ....

11. ΠΑΡΚΙΝΓΚ ....

12. ΚΑΦΕΤΕΡΙΑ ....

And now Greek words, alas spelled in Greek, which you should be able to recognise or at least guess.

1. ΕΓΩ ....
2. ΚΑΦΕΣ ....
3. ΚΕΝΤΡΟ ....
4. ΘΕΑΤΡΟ ....
5. ΠΡΟΒΛΗΜΑ ....
6. ΠΡΟΡΑΜΜΑ ....
7. ΙΣΤΟΡΙΑ ....
8. ΦΩΤΟΓΡΑΦΙΑ ....
9. ΤΗΛΕΦΩΝΟ ....
10. ΑΕΡΟΠΛΑΝΟ ....

Very useful words, all of them.

Now you are supposed to not only decipher them but also to pronounce them!!!! If for some reason, linguistics is not your forte or for that matter not even remotely of some interest to you, well then ask a Greek who can read to pronounce them for you.

If I feel like it, or if the book needs a few more pages, whichever comes first, I may add a few more practice words at the end.

How could I <u>ever</u> forget. ΤΟΥΑΛΕΤΤΑ pronounced TOO-A-LET-A is of course THE most important one. It means WC, bathroom or lavatory or even the loo, the john, or whatever you call it. The very word with a slight interogative inflection (?) will ellicit a pointed finger to the right direction.

Because you are doing so well so far, I have decided to give you a few very handy phrases that could make your life just a bit easier as a BONUS of course, free, at no extra cost whatsoever to you. Isn't that nice?
Phonetically at that for your convenience.

POO EENE	Where is ......
POSO KANEE	How much is it?
OHI	No
BAH	No
BAH???	Is that right?
THEN KATALAVA	I didn't understand.

PA-PA-PA-PA-PA	Never
POLÝ KALÓ	Very good
SUPER	Super
GIA KLÁMATA	Terrible
THÉLO	I want
NEH	Yes
PARAKALÓ	Please
THANKS	Thanks

If you have any difficulties, try to talk to a young person, even a ten-year-old. Public schools have only just introduced foreign languages into the school curriculum, however 97% of Greek children study English in private schools and well they should. At any rate, you may not understand the response, particularly if it's in English or Greenglish, just rely then on the hand, arm and body movements, pointing fingers and other indications.

And a few letter combinations that sound nothing like they should.

OY = OO as in TOO

AI = E as in BET

EI = I as in PIECE   ALSO OI= I as in PIECE

AY = AV as in AVIATION

Humor in signs like the following,
for Restorants, City Genters,
Motorbeikes to rent, Meales,
Bageris, Beauty Saloons
Spagetti and winning Kilometers.
I wonder how you do that!

22

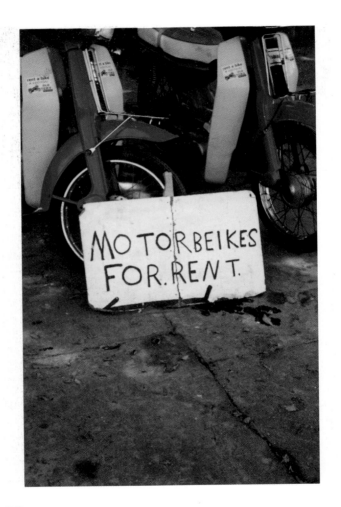

Aramis ←

ΚΑΦΕΔΕΣ	COFFIES
ΑΝΑΨΥΚΤΙΚΑ	SOFT DRINKS
ΠΟΤΑ	DRINKS COCTAILS
ΠΑΣΤΕΣ	PASTRIES
ΠΑΓΩΤΑ	ICE CREAMS
ΠΡΩΙΝΑ	BREAKFAST
ΠΙΤΣΑ	PIZZA
ΜΑΚΑΡΟΝΑΔΑ	- SPAGETTI

26

CITY CENTER?

"Winn"? They must mean "win"
but so what? It still makes no sense.

29

II

WHERE-TO

PLACES TO VISIT IF YOU WANT TO PRETEND YOU ARE NOT A TOURIST

ATHENS

Here I will not mention the obvious and absolute MUSTS, like the Acropolis on any day but preferably on a smogless one. Instead, I must tell you about Filopappou, the hill which is across the Acropolis and within walking distance from it with a small white monument on its top.

A short climb up the quiet hill full of pines is a welcome respite from the din of the city. Not only from the top, but from virtually every spot you choose along the way, you'll have exquisite views of the Acropolis and the Parthenon, most of them framed by the pine trees that surround you. From the very top you have a stunning view of the city from the coast to the mountains north.

You will hardly meet anyone else when a few hundred yards away, on the sacred hill itself, thousands of people are either waiting in long lines to get in, or are crowding the hill itself.

Filopappou is a true delight and I do hope that by writing this I do not contribute to changing its serenity and its beauty.

The Plaka and the flea market are great in the winter.

During the summer, day or night, it's like going to the county fair. If you like a fair-like atmosphere fine, but then most likely you would not be reading this book. I'd rather be sitting in a "koutouki" - that's what Athenians call some neighborhood taverns. Don't ask me what it means, the closest I've come to a translation is "tree stump" but I can tell you a couple of things about what it is. In the midst of endless apartment houses, deafening noise and poisoned air, the koutoukia (plural) are a haven, a tranquil contradiction of the cement that Athens is today. In the least expected places down town, you find yourself in a country tavern, not a contrived, artificially made one - the Greeks wouldn't stand for that, or it would not be a koutouki - but an authentic, honest to goodness, down to earth place. Somehow they have survived the onslaught of cement, perhaps, as incongruous as it may seem, because the property itself is too strange a configuration to build a "modern" apartment on.

Their outside yard is congested with old wooden tables that at night remain empty till about 10.30. By 11.00 you probably will not find a place to sit. Some wooden wine barels on one side against the apartment wall are indeed full of wine. Overhead the trelliss is covered with grape heavy vines, in the summer only of course. The tables and chairs must be at least 100 years old. The small building that houses the kitchen is well over that age but freshly painted a bright white. In the rear, the unisex restroom with its makeshift red door, is hardly big enough to fit a full size adult human and you must lower your head

34

to get in if you are over 5 feet tall.

 The owner-waiter-assistant cook will not rush over to seat
you, you just find your way and choose a table of your
liking. Sooner or later, depending on how busy they are
at the time, a young boy will make sure that your table has
a new plastic sheet over it and a basket with bread, paper
napkins and silverwar thrown in it. He will disappear as
quickly as he appeared.Eventually the owner-waiter-cook
will come to your table and either deposit a menu-bill in
front of you and leave or ask you for your order assuming
that you already know the menu. Should anyone ask
what's available he will begrudgingly tell you, well to be
fair you may catch him in a good mood day, not too busy
consequently more hospitable even flippant and
humorous. The food is not ordered with the sort of order
you may be accustomed to. You begin with the
appetisers not individually but after a consensus with
your friends and you and the waiter. The appetisers are
served in small plates and if your group has a favorite one,
say giant beans, you could order two or more portions.

 So many salads, so many potatoes, so many souvlakis - a
delicious if unpredictable meat, seasoned and marinated
and grilled to overly well done, just shy of almost burned.
DELICIOUS. (Food descriptions will follow separately.)
The wine is retsina and although some have unflatteringly
likened it to kerosene, it complements the ambience
much better than Chardonay. It is a lot less expensive,
and has almost the same effect. And I do say almost

because I cannot compromise this setting with stemmed wine glasses and french wine. This is short, stubby glass, retsina country. Some tables away, around midnight, somebody unveils a guitar and the group sings in less than operatic voices, strange, melodic tunes which contagiously everyone, including our owner-waiter, hums along with. How could anyone have Chardonay with this?

The food arrives promptly. Our waiter has both arms and hands loaded with 10-15 plates, a feat that deserves an ovation at any county fair, but gets none here. Honestly, I saw no thumb in the salad plate. With incredible skill and artistry if not finesse, the plates are set on the table in any order that can be managed without stacking them too much. Some empty plates are set and we are ready.

Not being a food critic, I lack the usual vocabulary that describes food so well in newspapers and which I seldom read. To me food is to be eaten, not described. I do like Woody Allen's "hypnotically seductive" or was it "seductively hypnotic" wine description however. He is not a food critic either.

At any rate I know what I like. Brains for example I didn't like. (Read this as you wish.) They are not as tasty at the locals seem to think and their cholesterol count is 1013647 somethings (SMGs) per 1/8th a teaspoon.

But I digress. The salad is crisp, the feta as good as I've had anywhere, the souvlaki superb, the condosouvli (not a tongue twister) magnificent, the dolmathes excellent, the giant beans incredible, and the music wonderful. I am fresh out of superlatives, only adverbs left. Oh, how could I forget the wine? It was indeed "hypnotic YET seductive" and for that matter so was the whole evening.

There are several koutoukia in Athens. The one I really like is H ΛΕΥΚΑ -ee léfka= the poplar tree on ODOS MAVROMIHALI 121 and VOULGAROCTONOU. If this isn't a mouthful I don't know what is. It is relatively easy to find if you follow **Ypokratous next to the Library on Panepistimiou st.** for about 20 blocks and make a left on Voulgaroctonou. Don't fret it. These are really short blocks and an easy walk from the Library.

So what else is worth doing in Athens besides eating? There are many guide books unhumorously describing several interesting small museums as well as the large Archaeological Museum on Patission Street. I will not try to do something others have done so well and so expensively. This is not after all the reason you bought my book. I must mention only one of them because it is out of the way, it is not quite a "museum", you can combine it with a visit to some remarkable caves, and it is, in my not so humble opinion, one of the jewels of Greece. It is a relaxing thing to do as well, even if relaxing is not on your schedule.

To get there you'll need to take the bus to PEANIA or Paiania. You do that from the terminal at ODOS MAVROMATEON near PEDION TOU AREOS just a few blocks away from the Archaeological Museum on Odos Patision. It really is no terminal, just a street that happens to be wide enough to accomodate the parking of buses. Just to make sure though, check with your concierge because such things have a habit of changing without prior notices, sometimes twice a year.

Peania is a small village in Messogia, behind Mount Ymmitos, northeast of Athens. It is a short ride, about an hour or so depending on traffic, delivery trucks, greek drivers, demonstrations and the driver's mood. Once in Peania, ask or follow the signs to the VORRES ESTATE. Ion Vorres, if he is in town, will host you through his sprawling residence, after you have visited his adjacent small but noteworthy, modern Greek art collection,

38

housed in a well-designed building. The house complex used to be abandoned stables some years back. It is now one of the most exciting places I've ever visited. Being a Scorpio, not by choice I assure you, I am not prone to compliments unless they are truly merited. Well, Voress's place deserves all the superlatives I can muster so I won't bore you with them.

The various buildings have retained the original Greek folk architecture and combine it with unintrusive and complementary elements such as large windowed walls and sky lights for today's living. The complex includes new sections that were added around the stables, retaining the originals' look, and creating a magnificent, meandering courtyard with natural rather than contrived, indigenous landscaping. A variety of items spanning 2500 years decorate the courtyard. Oil stones, used to crush olives and produce oil, are placed in recesses in the stone walls. Ancient pieces lie here and there, casually, as though they belonged. Inside the house the various rooms that have hosted many a royalty and dignitaries, are decorated by many authentic pieces. Byzantine icons, old wooden doors, the very valuable antiques next to common old pieces are juxtaposed in an extraordinary eclectic, fascinating way. Mr Vorres, a delightful host, will explain many of the pieces' history, how he came upon them, how he acquired them, why he decided to use them and in which way and tell you some of his remarkable ideas on the merits of local architecture. He will do this in several languages, depending on the ethnic composition of his small group, switching from one language to another as effortlessly as if he were only speaking one.   Phone 664 4771, Saturday-Sunday 10.00 - 2.00.

The taxi drive up to the caves is very short but spectacular. You should be able to find a taxi at the village square or PLATEEA phonetically in Greek. The whole grape growing valley unrolls before your eyes as your cab goes up the steep route to the cave gate. This area is called MESSOGIA or Inland because it is 4- 5 miles away from the sea. It is famed for its good retsina, the inimitable Greek wine.

Once in the caves, you'll be overwhelmed by the stalactites and stalagmites that have taken millions of years to form. I was told that they were the largest in the world. I am not sure that this is true, or that it is not the wish of the Greeks living in a small country, to have something that is the "EST" in the world.

Lunch in any of the village's several tavernas is a welcome respite before the bus ride back to the city. Make sure you check the bus schedule and know ahead of time where the bus stop is.

Another day trip out of the ordinary is to PARNITHA. That's where the casino is as well, but that is not its real asset. The bus ride is again about an hour long, give or take a few irate drivers.

This mountain is at the north-western rim of the LEKANOPEDIO which is the basin that contains Athens, Piraeus and their suburbs, 4,000,000 inhabitants they tell me and 1,500,000 motor vehicles - it sure feels like twice as many - excluding mopeds and motorcycles, of which I am absolutely sure there are zillions.

Back on the mountain, however. Unlike what one expects or imagines about Greece, its mountains are every bit as majestic as the ALPS in certain areas. Greece is not only the sea, the sun, the islands, some 2,000 of them I was told. Parnitha is a tranquil, alpine, high mountain with pines - the Norway Christmas tree variety I mean. I've seen snow up there in April and regardless of seasons, its many paths and trails are wonderful for those who like hiking and have some stamina left after walking the streets of Athens.

There are some more interesting locations in and around Athens but if you forgive me, I must save some material for the next "new and improved" edition or the next books. Besides, this is enough for you to do this time around.

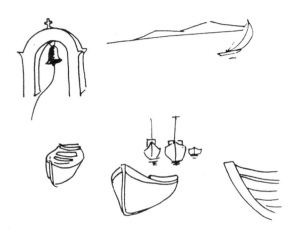

AWAY FROM ATHENS

Real writers and poets have sung the praises of the greek islands. I cannot outdo them nor will I try. Rather, I'd like to offer some out of the way places, not too touristy, fully aware that doing so jeopardises their purity and tranquility. I am assuming of course that this book will be read and that some people may actually do what I am suggesting herewith. A lot of ifs at best. Let's just hope then, that you'll be one of the first.

The whole world has become one mega tourist place, save the dozen or so danger zones and I for one like to avoid such places where people are crowding one another as though they were in an Athens trolley ar at peak time. As crowded as Greece gets in the summer, if summer is the only time you can travel, there are still some oases. If you can avoid summer altogether, then I would suggest spring or fall, otherwise known as the shoulder seasons. Some of the hotels aren't open yet, or they may have closed and all the fery boat lines aren't in full swing but by and large Greece is an untouched fruit bowl then and you can take your pick. In July and August however you'll thank me should you listen to me or curse the moment you were born if you don't.

From the islands I'll choose just two for now. There are a few more and I am looking for them. I'll keep you posted. You keep buying my books!!!

The Cyclades are a group of well travelled islands to the south east of Athens. They are regularly serviced by several boats departing from Piraeus. Some of them have airports and also a relatively new, fast, therefore more expensive catamaran boat. They are barren and austere if you compare them to the Sporades to the north, but they do have a charm of their own. If we leave the fabled and overdone Myconos alone or just for a day trip, I recommend Syros with its stately neoclassical architecture and absolutely enchanting Ano Syros, where you might see two tourists on any given day in the summer and none in the spring or fall, and its a photographer's paradise. Ano Syros happens to be high up on top of one of the two hills that dominate Ermoupolis, the island's capital. The views are indeed breathtaking, this is no exaggeration cliche, just a normal one. You can get there by car or taxi or even hike if you have strong constitution.. Just remember that the way back is all down hill. There are no cars in the area itself not even mopeds thank God. None of them can negotiate Ano Syros's narrow staired winding streets. All transportation is on foot or by donkey. The taxi will leave you just outside its gates and you'll wander around toward the top and the Catholic church. One feels as though he (or she) is intruding on the villagers as they go about their daily chores, leaving doors and windows wide open. You can spend several hours there and later, once you have left it you know that you must return, perhaps at a different time of the day or maybe at sunset or at nite to eat at the Ano Syros's only tavern,PIATSA which offers not only a spectacular view but also a character of an owner-chef-waiter and the entertainment of the locals singing the songs of Vamvakaris who used to live a few doors away.

If you like the sea, -silly to be on an island if you don't- Syros has wonderful clean beaches like Achladi Agathopes or Delagratsia, all a short distance by bus from Ermoupolis.

At night the best little bar in all of Greece appropriately called TO BARAKI, literally litle bar, is an outdoor place with its little tables and chairs under the trees in the courtyard of an old house just left of the magnificent neo-classical city hall in the main square of the town. The owner plays piano around one or two A.M., and he is good at it. Even if he wasn't, his repertoire is excellent. More frequently than not the crowd will join in a hum-along of good old tunes.

Besides TO BARAKI, there is another late night spot approprietly called THE BEST in perfect.....Greek.It is a music bar, located next to the NOMARXIA -county court house- on the water, a most romantic spot with little tables on a deck that overlooks Ta Vaporia district, with its stately buildings above the water up the hill. On a moonlit night it is the best place to be in Greece and even outside of Greece whether you are with your love -interest or not. The time to go there is after 1:00 am. They usually stay open till 4 or 5 am and sometimes till daylight! You can even ask them to change the music if it is not totally to your liking, and depending on the owner's mood they may just do it!

This would make a perfect end for the day, but I have to tell you where to go before TO BARAKI. In Syros you go to a fish tavern. Two of them are noteworthy simply because I cannot forget their names. UGLY'S is one (AS-HEE-MOS) and LAZY'S is the other (TEM-BE-LIS). Regardless of whether they are worthy of their respective names, their food is always fresh and tasty.

Should you want to be cosmopolitan for a day, you can take a day trip to Myconos. Small boats will take you there in an hour in the morning and return you in the afternoon for a small price.

áno Syros

Of the west coast, on the Ionian Sea, is the small island of PAXOS just two hours away from the famous and cosmopolitan Corfu. The island is so small - only seven miles long and two miles wide - that with the exception of a couple of modest hotels, accommodations are self-catering in villas by the sea or in apartments and private homes, sort of Greek bed and breakfast inns.

The air in Paxos and its culture is entirely different from that of the rest of Greece and the Aegean Islands. There are seven islands on the west coast, well actually a few more uninhabited ones, called Eptanissa. Being on the west coast they were never occupied by the Ottoman Empire as was most of the rest of the land for about 400 years. Their proximity to Italy has had an influence on the food, music, language, architecture and a bunch more things I won't bother you with here.

Gaios is the capital and the only place in the three villages where you might find the sign of a bar. Lakka, just across from Corfu in the north has a perfectly protected bay and a few fish taverns. Loggos, in between the two, is a small charming fishing village popular subject for artists, great and small. It too has wonderful fish taverns, which is great, if you like loads of fresh fish.

No historic monuments decorate the island, but there are a lot of relaxing things to do. Plenty of boats for hire or on regular runs, make it easy to go to remote coves for swimming, or visit the west side and its limerock cliffs and crystal clear, turquoise waters.

The inland landscape is quite different. Gnarled olive trees dominate the terrain and lend their color and shade to the scene. Paxos is a hiker's dream or paradise, depending on which cliche you prefer. The paths will take you through olive groves, old olive presses and windmills. To make things easier, you could take a bus from Gaios to Moungelatika or Kondogiannitika and from there a pleasant hike down hill ll the way to the sea for lunch in a fish tavern of course.

A side trip can take you to Antipaxos, a still smaller neighboring island with 5 inhabitants I was told. Voutoumi is the main beach and the busiest at high season. Yet just around the small cape, Mesovrica is quiet and pristine.

Another day trip will take you to the cosmopolitan madness that Corfu is in August. You can even stay overnight if you wish to participate in the nigh time disco entertainment or return to civilisation in Paxos.

P.S. I thought of putting a small section on **shopping** in this chapter of WHERE TO, but I gave up the idea because there are too many tourist shops that offer pretty much the same things. I do have a paragraph or two in the HOW TO chapter.

II

WHAT TO
and what not to

WHAT TO EAT

Although I am not sure that Greek drinks (wines, spirits, ouzo) would be considered nectar by visitors who have sometimes likened them to less savory liquids (kerosene, turpentine) I AM sure that Greek food is indeed ambrosia, if prepared properly. The food may well be the reason "The Gods chose Greece" which is the current slogan of the Greek Tourist Organisation.

I will recommend that a visitor tastes a variety of traditional dishes in good restaurants or tavernas in Greece, or anywhere for that matter. An attempt to reproduce them at home I would not recommend unless you are really into cooking and don't mind spending the better part of the summer in the kitchen. There is no such thing as Greek fast food, regardless what the various Gyro-Kings and ...... Souvlasseries may want you to think. Do not be offended by, nor should you try a number of preparations which include various internal organs of animals, unless you have an affinity for such things as liver, intestines, stomachs, gall bladders and other bladders, brains, etc. Stick to more traditional things that contain ground meat, vegetables, fish and a variety of meat cuts, unrelated to meat cuts elsewhere. The greeks, as in everything else, have their own inimitable way, which .... foodwise at least works.

DIGRESSION #1

An infinite source of entertainment is solving ..... the
menu. Written most of the time in low-Greenglish may
well have you rolling in the aisles. Below is a modest
example of some of the "things" I have noticed this past
week alone. Space is provided for the answers. Those
of you getting 3 correct answers are guaranteed not to
starve!

LAM TSOPS
BIFTEKI
SPAGETI
COCTAILS
BREKFAST
SANDWHITS
EGGFISH
MEAT BOLS
SPESIALS

Back to the real thing though. We shall start with WHAT
TO EAT for ..... the **NOT AT ALL ADVENTUROUS.**

The easy way out, and maybe the cheapest, is PASTA,
only be sure not to call it "pasta" lest you be directed to a
pastry shop. You see, pasta in Greek is MACARONI, and
pastries - super yummy not to mention absolutely divine,
wonderful etc. - and pastries as I was saying is pasta.

Please don't ask why. I do not want to make this book too long and therefore too expensive. So if you stick with macaroni then or spaghetti you are pretty safe. Not only that, but Greeks are really better at pastas and sauces than the Italians. Sorry to my Italian f riends but it is true. But to add injury to mere insult, so is the Greek pizza, which as luck would have it, is called pizza in Greece as well, better than its New York counterpart. Of course you can tell me that that doesn't mean much, but anyway ..... pizza in Greece, partially due to economics is better because they use Gouda instead of the innocuous Mozzarella. You see not only does Gouda have a real personality, whereas Mozzarella is BLAh cubed (did those of you into mathematics notice the pun?) but it is also cheaper in Greece. Greek pizza is almost always great.

If you object to the whole notion and tell me that you didn't go, or come, all the way to Greece to taste Italian food, let me remind you that I am addressing this section to the least adventurous of you and let me assure you that surprising things are coming up.

A Greek salad is always great and a reasonably easy thing to do, so no restaurant, regardless of its mediocrity, can foul it up too much. You may notice differences in taste and they have to do more with the produce, oil and cheese in that particular area. The cheese is feta and it goes - usually - with the peasant salad or HO-RIA-TIKI. If you don't like feta, then you can have a tomato and onion salad or a tomato and cucumber one. Produce is fresh and tasty in the summer time.

 BEEF-TE-KI is a lightly seasoned Greek hamburger and it beats MacDonald's and Burger King's anytime even Wendy's. Try some lemon on it.

SOMEWHAT ADVENTUROUS (but timid)

 YEE-ROS, SOU-VLA-KI, MOO-SA-KA, PAS-TEE-TSO, now we're getting somewhee.

 YEE-ROS or GYROS - a sandwich or is it a sandwitch or a sandouits (I am forgetting my languages) made up of an undetermined yet delicious meat, cooked or broioled rather on a vertical spit for effect, lightly seasoned with salt, oregano, salt, spices, salt, oregano, salt, spices and salt. Marinated in lemon and oil - I think, but I am not absolutely certain - sprinkled with onions, tomatoes and TZA-DZI-KI (a yogurt and chives and something else concoction) wrapped in a slightly toasted and very slightly buttered PITA which is in turn wrapped in paper, so as only your hands and torso get greasy and not your entire body.

 SOUVLAKI - several variations exist. Some shopkeepers will try to pass GYROS as SOUVLAKI, then again others won't. The variety I like is the mini-shish-kabob on a small stick of bamboo. I can literally eat dozens of them. Presented pretty much like Yeeros in fastfood places or

54

as a main dish in uptown spots, it is as delicious either way.

MOOSAKA and PASTEETSO - Greek versions and variations of lasagna, or it could well be the other way around. Basically, macaroni with layers of ground beef, topped with bechamel sauce and cooked in the oven. Moosaka - careful, the accent on KA, lest they take you for a tourist - also contains a bottom layer or two of eggplant, depending on how expensive it is that time of the year, and a layer or two of potatoes. Also DELICIOUS.

Here I am debating whether I should mention a couple of other things but perhaps this is enough to take care of you for a few days at any rate. The good old standby, french fries or fried potatoes or chips to the Brits are always great in Greece. That along with a good salad ought to do until you are ready to become

MODESTLY ADVENTUROUS

KEF-TE-DES, SOU-DZOU-KIA (not a Japanese car), DOL-MA-DES

The first two are nothing more than yummy meat balls, different only in the light spices used and in shape and also the fact that soudzoukia or soudzoukakia are served in a tomato sauce. Dolmades are strange looking, ground beef and rice mixture wrapped in a vine leaf - who else would have thought of this but a Greek? - and doused with an egg and lemon divinely delicious sauce. If the vine leaves are tender this indeed is food for the Gods. Am I repeating "delicious" too often? Well it just might be the reason I always gain several kilos when in Greece.

DO-MA-TES YIE-ME-STES

Stuffed tomatoes or peeperies yiemeestes, stuffed peppers, usually stuffed with ground beef and rice and surrounded by a thin, oily, incredible tomato sauce, and sometimes accompanied by baked potatoes cooked in the same pot. I could live on this for a whole year or even more.

By now you must have gathered that I am writing about some of my favorite things. Indeed so far I am. Sooner or later though, we are really going exotically native, so why not spice things up a little bit right now with suggestions for those who are.....

QUITE ADVENTUROUS

KA-LA-MA-RIA or KALAMARAKIA

Squid, deep fried to what else but golden brown to steal a phrase from Wendy's or was it Pizza Hut's menu. Delicious once again for those of you who like sea creatures with ten arms and long soft bodies. Now if you

56

have preference for sea creatures with only eight arms that also act as legs and feet, then you must order OCTOPUS or HTA-PO-DI in Greek. Both squid and octopus when small are much tastier. Octopus is served as an appetizer - if you can imagine that. I am sure it has quite the opposite effect on some - sometimes grilled, cold, with oil and vinegar. OUZO, the anisete Greek absenth, is the drink that traditionally goes along and complements the Aegian taste.

Moving right along, and strictly for the garlic lover, is SKOR-DA-LIA an ambrosia of a garlic dip served in a small bowl as a complement to some foods like fried cod. Its only disadvantage being that it emits strange and sometimes uncomfortable odors - for those nearby - from all parts of the body for rather lengthy periods of time. My last venture into skordalia was during the Truman Administration and I swear that I still feel its after effects. They tell me, however, that it is good for the heart and a good thing it is because I have had several nose attacks. And I do get them frequently when riding the buses in Athens. You see the Greeks believe in those home remedies and indulge for medicinal purposes. Garlic is also used liberally in a number of other preparations except perhaps banana splits, which is a good place to stop and get into foods for the

EXTREMELY   ADVENTUROUS
or congenitally insane

(over)

For this category I have some humdingers compared only to Eskimo haute cuisine.No inference or implication here but well seasoned maggets are not my ....cup of tea.

KO-KO-RE-TSI, PA-TSAS, SPLIN-AN-DE-RO should be enough to give you an idea. There are plenty more but I must have material for the next book.

Kokoretsi is a very good looking food - deceptively so - you frequently see in spits horizontally rotating, divinely smelling and on the surface appearing absolutely YUMMY. Contents: small intestines of unfortunate if undetermined animals, colons, including the sphyncter muscle I believe, slowly grilled to ...... perfection, of course, and hopefully having previously been cleaned very well. Half jobs in these parts of the body just don't cut it for me.

Patsas is a favorite of Xenihtides. They are those individuals who having been entertained all night long, find themselves extremely hungry around four or five in the morning. Not many places are open then so somebody sometime ago thought it would be worth trying to get rid of the only parts of the animal not used during the sane and sober eating hours. Lo and behold it became a huge success and the thing to do before going to bed for the day. I am not so sure that it would have met with nearly as much acceptance as a normal meal at normal hours. Let me explain why. Patsas is a soup-like concoction, whose basic ingredients are stomachs of small and large edible I hope, animals. I can only suspect that they too are cleaned prior to cooking. What else can I say?

Splinandero. SPLI-NAN-DE-RO. A sausage stuffed with hearts, gall bladders, lives, ears, feet, spleens, kidneys and voltage regulators of animals hereafter called "the substance" and in reality not very different in ingredients than the good old American hot dog. However, the substance has not been pulverized to a civilised if unrecognisable mush and it is spiced differently. It's all a matter of perception I guess.

I hope that this is enough for now. Depending on how you classify yourself try the corresponding foods. You will not be disappointed.

Most restaurants, forgive me, restorants I meant to say, offer ready made dishes - **e-teema** - that you can inspect in the kitchen, or **tis oras** that you order if you are willing to wait a while. Things like steaks and a variety of other steak-like cuts only found in Greece such as FEE-LE-TO or bon-fillet which is fillet mignon are TIS ORAS. They are a safe if expensive bet for the meat-n-potatoes person. They are wonderful and I do suggest a little lemon on them. Try it, it sure beats Worcestershire - or something that looks like it - sauce. You cannot ask for rare or medium or anything but well done, or done till the cook thinks they are. Trust him.

If you like coffee during or after, forget it unless you are in the uptown area that caters to Americans at "let's get the damn yankeest" prices. For coffee and or dessert - fondly spelled desert - you must go to a ZA-HA-RO-PLAS-TÍO after the taverna. I can guarantee to you that you have never tasted pastries as good as the Greek ones. Greece being at the crossroads between the Middle East and Europe and being inhabited by people whose teeth are sweet has the best pastry chefs in the world having been influenced by both sides and having adapted for the Greek taste. So enjoy your nescafe or your Greek cofee and a fine piece of pastry or PASTA. Remember?

Speaking of Greek coffee, EL-LI-NI-KÓS CAFFÉS, you can order it in one of several ways, for the sake of brevity, GLEE-KÓS is sweet MÉ-TRI-OS is semi-sweet and SKE-TOS which is plain. Careful. Sip it. Don't drink it to the bottom because the bottom third is grounds and it doesn't taste so great.
Besides GREEK COFFEE there is also NÉSCAFE or, in a rare display of efficiency and economy also called NES which is no more than a cup of hot water and an envelop of instant coffee. There is also filtered coffee which is somewhat closer to the American norm only here it is called...FRENCH or Gallikòs or FÍLTROU.
A coffee very popular here in the summer but less known elsewhere is FRAPPE' which is iced coffee . Iced tea is not known as yet but a FRAPPE can take its place nicely, particularly if you don't expect it to be too iced. A good

FRAPPE is supposed to be so well shaken, that half the glass is ...foam. So you get a taste of coffee foam as well!!

I think this about does it for this chapter. If I think of anything else, there is enough space left on this page. If I don't, then I'll put a cute little sketch- pen and ink drawing- below.

IV

HOW TO

SHOPPING

As I mentioned previously , in the WHERE TO chapter I will mention a few things here about how to shop. I put nothing in that chapter for a number of reasons. Most tourists buy touristy things , I don't. The most touristy thing I ever bought is a T-shirt here and there and only if I was impressed by its design somehow. I also must admit that I am interested in quaint "local" things such as tools,Kitchen utensils, music and a number of things that I have never been able to locate in 'tourist' shops and if I do they are seldom of the quality I'd want.So if you are interested in touristy things such as mementos of your trip, Knic-knacks (is this how it is spelled?) hedious little samples and reproductions of "art"and so on, there are litterally millions of such shops all over the land.Suit your own needs and taste and pocketbook.There are some good buys in gold and silver jewellry again "touristy" things, but also the world reknown master jeweller Ilias Lalaounis with pieces inspired from ancient designs has a beautiful if pricy shop on Odos Panepistimiou 6 in Athens.

So in this section I willgive you a few pointers on how to shop rather than what to or where to shop. On that issue I will only mention some shopping areas. The Plaka area is infested with "touristy" shops in Athens as are most central streets all over the country. Specifically in Athens if you are interested in some nice boutiques you go to Kolonaki. Ask directions near Syntagma square. It is just moments away on foot, up Odos Voukourestiou if you can pronounce it. A good shopping area is also in the northern suburb of Kiffisia, and another in the southern suburb of Glyfada by the sea.If shopping is your "thing" it may be worth your while to take an afternoon off and visit either of these areas. Your consierge will gladly direct you.

But I digress again ! Back to HOW TO shop. The key word here is BARGAIN. What do you mean you don't know how to ? Of course you do. You bargain every day of your life. You're just not accustomed to do it in a shop. Haven't you ever said to your son "Tommy you mow the lawn today and I"ll give you five dollars" ? And hasn't Tommy said " Daaaaaad it takes two whole hours to do it in this heat and besides what can you get nowadays for 5 bucks?"and you've said........ need I go on? Well you do the same kind of a thing in the shops here and you just might be surprised to find out that the shopkeeper might be more agreeable than your Tommy.So it is no different buying two T-shirts and a little statue than buying a car from a used car salesman. "What is your bottom price for me?" should become your standard phrase when shopping. Also the word "no" and Definately NO and Absolutely NO or simply NONONONONONONO and repeat the question, "I asked for the very bottom price". You'll be very surprised at the results. Frequently the more emphatic the NO, the lower the next price will be.Trust me, you just might be able to save enough to buy 20 of these little books for the "folks back home"on a purchase of a few T-shirts or a couple of little statues. Good luck.

HOW TO GET A TAXI

Well it may be a simple matter elsewhere and to be honest it isn't that difficult outside of Athens where the taxis are grey. In Athens the taxis are yellow but they are no taxis as you know them. They are mini buses-capacity 4 people-and the taxi drivers understandably do not like to get groups because they only get a single fare . If they take singles here and there going roughly in the same direction, then they can charge multiple fares and come out way ahead. It is slightly illegal but the state never fusses too much with such insignificant details. Matter of fact they do not fuss too much with significant details either. This creates a small problem for the tourist if one happens to be some place other than the entrance of one's hotel. You must stand at the edge of the sidewalk, or even out in the street if you are insanely brave and wave your arms wildly when a yellow vehicle approaches. A few feet away you start screaming your destination. Careful to hide your partner, if you have one, or else the cabby most likely will not stop for two. You may be lucky and get a cab in reasonable time, say before the next presidential elections, yet you may not be.

HOW TO DRIVE IN GREECE

DON'T.
Nobody else does either.

HOW TO WALK

You may already know how to walk, but I will guarantee that you do not know how to walk in Greece.

To begin with, one would surmise that one should be able to walk with reasonable safety and ease on city sidewalks, or pavements as you Brits like to call them.Not so in Greece. The sidewalks are (a) for trees (b) for moped parking (c) for car parking (d) for moped riding.So if you must walk make sure you do it cautiously and carefully always watching over your shoulder even when not passing, and always glancing at the pavement because it suddenly may not be there or if it is, it may not be in the form one would normally expect.

HOW TO FIND ROAD AND DIRECTIONAL SIGNS

Look behind or inside nearby trees

HOW TO BOARD PUBLIC TRANSPORT

Regardless of the means be it a bus or a ferry boat or an airplane my suggestion is simple yet incredibly effective. Just PUSH. The bigger you are the more authority your PUSH will have.When PUSHING is not effective enough then SHOVE. In one simple word. You do know after all the wise old dictum " when in Greece do as the Greeks'

HOW TO GET THERE, SAY A FEW MORE THINGS,

A GET ALONG IN GENERAL

Getting around in Greece may not be as formidable as it appears at first.It might be just a bit frustrating requiring one to muster all the patience available, even take an advance on next year's. One way out, if you are willing to spend some money, is to hire a car AND a driver who has had plenty of experience in Greek driving. Reference here must be made to GREEK DRIVING AND OTHER

OXYMORA. You do know of course what an oxymoron is, don't you? Well just in case, an oxymoron is a mutually exclusive phrase, an impossibility such as "plastic silverwear". My extremely unauthoritative guide on why a sane person should not drive in Greece will convince you to hire a driver, even if you can't afford one. You are taking a risk of puting your (brake) foot through the floor at any rate.

The other option is to get a taxi, if you can find one. They are yellow as in other parts of the world, so people can locate them easily. However, Greek cab drivers are capricious enough and too independent to take you where YOU want to go. They prefer to take you where THEY want to go, whether you want to go there or not, and more likely than not charge you about as much as your plane ticket to get here in the first place. But it is an alternative to taking the public, overloaded transportation and frustration system. Your best bet within cities is to walk, even if you are not accustomed to it, try to get used to it again.

If you must, and only then, use public transportation and you are fortunate enough to find someone who knows where you want to go and how to get there,(which number bus, and where it makes its stops) make sure you buy your ticket in advance from a kiosk and validate it once you are on the vehicle if you can reach the machine and if the machine is working. I could never figure out if you validate it or you INvalidate it. At any rate, here is a handy explanation of the various public conveyances city and country, land and sea, but not air. I have not had the guts to try that yet.

ATHENS

<u>Trolleys</u> - large yellow weird looking things
They will take you between two points when not on strike or disrepair. Trolleys, being electrically operated and driven by what appears to be the rookies of the profession, start and stop very suddenly and unexpectedly. So make sure that you hold onto something at all times, lest you unwillingly become extremely intimate with someone you may not even care to shake hands with or even smile at.

<u>Blue Buses</u> - bluish looking large mobile boxes of pre-renaissance vintage, commonly referred to as LEO-FO-RI'O
They stop wherever you see a bunch of people loitering impatiently in the general environs of a small blue sign with illegible yellow letters on it or even a small sticker advertising something or someone.

<u>The Underground</u> - well part of the way anyhow, known as E-LEC-TRI-COS (Main station at OMONIA but can also be taken at MONASTIRAKI at the flea market square near PLAKA.)
It will take you from Athens to Piraeus where the ferry-boats are and very close to them. Or if you want to go to the northern suburbs through several stops, and beggars you can get to Kifissia, a nice place indeed for pastry shops, good shopping, and some good restaurants. Kifissia is a good place to spend some time away from the smog and traffic of the city.

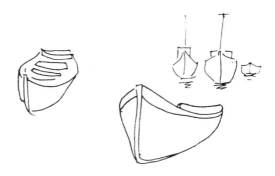

TO THE ISLANDS

To get to the islands you must either fly - many of them have places that resemble airports and many of them actually do have airports - or go by boat which could really be half the fun and then again a frustrating experience should there be no place to sit for five hours. Monday through Thursday travel in the summer time, may be less frightening.

Ferry-Boats. These are known in Greek as FE'-RY-BOTS. Most of them depart from Piraeus. Buy a first class ticket if you can afford it. If you are a student or of that age and want to associate with people of your age still buy a first class ticket if the trip is longr than four-five hours. You can always go to third class from first but the reverse is not always true, just sometimes and only after ticket inspections and if the boat is not too overloaded. Hold onto your tickets for those inspections. Also careful on how to board those ...things. There is no separate entry for passengers and vehicles nor is there a certain order. You will be boarded and it might feel like you are being loaded, along with trucks of assorted sizes, screaming motorcycles, cars and even.....helicopters. I swear that this is no exaggeration and I do have a picture to prove it. You will be.....unloaded pretty much the same way, regardless of your ticket class.

Flying Dolphins. The DEL-FI'-NIA are hydrofoils which are much faster and a bit more expensive. They are good for short distances and you are assigned a seat like an airplane. If the winds are high they do not.....fly however. Of Russian technology, just thought you might want to know.

Catamarans. Some of the popular islands are now serviced by CA-TA-MA-RA'NS which are new, fast, good and expensive. If time is of importance and you still want to capture the aura and ambience of traveling through the islands the cats are good for you although a bit bumpy

LAND TRAVEL

There are two basic ways I sort of trust, and air travel which is unpredictable enough because the Great and Mighty OLYMPIC is a governmental monopoly, so by the time you combine government - and Greek government at that - with monopoly, permanent employees, who can never be fired lest they assassinate the Prime Minister, well you know what I mean. Suffice to say that if you have a ticket and for some whimsical reason - such as the pilot forgot it was June - Olympic decides not to fly, you do not get a full refund on domestic flights. On international flights of course they are bound by IATA regulations and they can't get away with stuff like that. But I digress.....

The two reasonably safe ways then, are by bus - coach to you from England - and by train. The buses that are connecting Greek cities towns and villages are not those wonderful, modern privately owned tourist buses that take groups around. No. They are those green looking things that you may recall around Disraelis's times. Yes, they are still here and doing reasonably well. They connect you with virtually any place you may want to visit and even with some places you may never have wanted to. Fortunately the days of traveling along with goats and their owners are gone, colorful as they were. In today's travel you may travel with a few chickens and the children of Atttila the Hun but not with goats, although on second thought it probably was preferable (goat co-travelers I mean).At any rate your friendly hotel-owner-consierge receptionsist-bellboy will direct you to the terminal, which is in such an ungodly place that you will need a taxi driver with a near genius IQ to find. So I will not bother you with addresses. For timetable information you could call 142 and you may reach somebody that if you really are nice to and pleading enough, they might feel sorry enough to give you the information you need. They too are permanent public employees seemingly having just learned to walk upright, as Woody Allen used to say.

Well, the train is not a great improvement but a little faster - if you are lucky. The information number is 145 and the terminal is near Omonia Square although I would not try to walk it. I used to think that "what the hell! it is not expensive ANYWAY". It used to be a good excuse. Unfortunately now it is ALSO expensive but it gets you there.

HOW TO DRESS

I debated whether to put this under this category or WHAT TO wear. But this chapter needed more beefing up my alter-editor said and I obeyed.

The obvious key here is the season. Not too brilliant a deduction. However this brings us to the climate of Greece at different times of the year. I will start with summer since most travelers are here in the summer and I sell more books then. Summers in Greece are very hot, but that too is relative. Traveling north from Africa you'll find Greece pleasant. Traveling south from say Finland you'll find it blazing hot here, but after all, this is the reason you came, the sea and the sun and maybe the sand as well. Temperatures in July and August are in the 30s Centigrade or 80s and 90s Fahrenheit but a hot wave will send them climbing to the 40s and 100s respectively, which may not be the best weather for walking around the Acropolis or for that matter anywhere. That's the time you want to find yourself on the islands where the temperatures are 5-10 degrees lower than Athens or some other inland locations.

The question may be already answered for you. Under the circumstances you wear as little as possible and as white as possible. I know that white gets dirty very easily but it is awfully comfortable. Light, cotton clothing is your best bet in the summer. The dry warm weather may require at times a very light jacket in the evening on the islands.

Spring and fall - April, May, some of June, late September and October - the weather is cooler and somewhat unpredictable. Heavier clothing will be needed even a rain jacket just in case. You may get some summer-like days and some winter-like ones. In the winter the temperatures can go as far as 0 or 32 F or even below that for brief periods and the cold is penetrating. It seldom lasts long and it could be followed by pleasant sunny days in the 20s or 60-70 range. Dress accordingly as clothing for some strange reason has become very expensive in recent years and you just do not want to get caught without a warm jacket unless you don't mind spending a large fortune for one locally.

One last yet extremely important matter. Take along -and use of course - VERY comfortable walking shoes for several reasons. First of all you will be doing more walking and climbing than normally. Secondly, you will be doing it in the most unlikely streets, sidewalks and hills. You'll remember me.

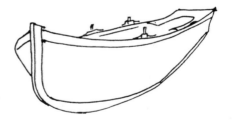

V

WHAT IS
and what isn't

In Greece frequently things are not what they seem to be at first or even at second and third glance. In other words"what you get is NOT necessairily what you see".
"How is that ?"you say. Well , a Cafeteria may not have coffee, a STOP sign means " slow down", a slip is men's underwear not women's, empathy means hate, system means chaos, method means pandemonium, and pandemonium means normal. See what I mean?

Consequently I deemed a chapter on GREEK STYLE DEFINITIONS a must. Here, I will include some handy information, such as phone numbers, money e.t.c. Kind of a catch-all and things-we- forgot section.

BILLS, TABS, TIPS at restaurants. Only "uptown" places in touristy areas accept credit cards. That goes for shops as well. So in a taverna expect to pay in cash. Leave only a few coins on the table for the cleaning boy , if you have any and if you feel like it -say 50 cents worth- because the tip to your waiter is INCLUDED in your bill !! This is always, not sometimes, even if the waiter is the owner. One of the few laws that inexplicably is religiously observed.

Speaking about money,this may be a good spot to talk to you about currency. The best places to get money exchanged is the banks, which of course are not open on week ends and which frequenly strike. The black market is all but gone now that Greece has become almost sane about exchange or actually was forced to, because of the EEC. (European Economic Community)

BILLS AND COINS   DRACHMA(S)

| 50 | BLUE small |

| 100 | RED |

| 500 | GREEN |

| 1000 | BROWN |

| 5000 | BLUE large |

(1) copper

(2) copper

(5) nickel

(10) nickel

(20) nickel-old
brass-new

(50) nickel-old
brass-new

(100) new-brass

RESTORÁN = Restaurant. There are many "types" of restaurants and eateries in general, so here is an attempt to desribe some of them

TAVÉRNA = Usually a very informal and folksy kind of place. The pricy ones distinguish themselves from the common ones by adding the adjective KOSMIKI which may mean "society" or social but it implies that the food and service are so good that only the "high"society can afford it. Sometimes there is music ,live that is and sometimes not. Fish and meat dishes available.

PSA-RO-TAVÉRNA = A fish tavern. Don't expect any meat dishes here.Salad, fried potatoes,appetizers however are available.

PSI-STA-RIÁ = A meat tavern. Don't expect any fish here. Just meats of different types almost always char-broiled or on a spit.

FASTFOONDÁDIKO= Any of the American style imitation adapted to Greektaste places mainly with souvlaki-gyros-chicken.However the BIG 3 Americans are here as well as PIZZA HUT and a few others.

ZA-HA-RO-PLA-STÍO =The most divine places on earth.This is in fact where you can have your coffee and the finest pastries on this earth. If you have a sweet tooth you will certainly satisfy it here.Try some tarts besides the well known BAKLAVA. But if that's what you want then do put the accent on the last syllable VA because that's where it belongs to begin with and you are not an obvious tourist.

KAFENION = Strictly for coffee and soft drinks and..... men. You'll notice that most of the KAFENIA are for males only. That's a man's refuge from the ....monotony of home life and a nagging wife. Some of them however allow women as well ,particularly in busy tourist areas.

There are a bunch more like the OUZERI for ouzo and appetizers or light eating only, PIZZERIA ,self explanatory,but I think 'nough on this subject.

All eateries are rated LUXURY, A,B,C,or A,B,Γ, not on the basis of food quality but rather amenities. The categories mentioned on the menu also indicate the price structure.

You may assume just by observing the Greek drivers that Greeks are impatient. Not so. You couldn't be further from the truth,believe me. The Greeks are indeed extremely patient people. They wait several years, twelve is not uncommon, for the installation of a..... telephone with no protest whatsoever. Not only that, but it is not uncommon either, to wait in line for several hours-2 to 4- just to pay the electricity bill or the water bill or the phone bill. Now tell me, are these impatient people? Surely not.

The current Berlitz Guide to Greece, says somewhere "schedules are largely theoretical". I like that. It's a wonderful understatement and very gently put. In Greece noon is NOT 12:00 o'clock Lord forbid.That's smack in the middle of the morning. Noon -MESIMÉRI or better yet MESIMERÅKI used to expand the time span politely, is between 2:00 and 6:00 p.m.,roughly. When you are told that your photos will be ready TO MESIMERAKI better clarify exactly what time at.....noon.

By thesame token AVRIO = tomorrow may not mean that at all. It may mean some time soon,which could be before the next Olympic Games.

Waving the palm of your hand at somebody in your friendly way indicating good-bye or "here we are" is not that at all in Greece. Here it is called a "moóntza and it means something equivalent to sending someone to a rather hot place known to all of us sinners.Or something that Woody Allen gently referred to as "be fruitful and multiply".

Do not worry too much if you are stared at considerably. Take it as a compliment because that's what it is. And all this time you thought it was rude, didn't you?

Never deny a Greek his hospitality. Take that cigarette if he offers it to you.He is extending his welcome and nothing more. And if it is an ouzo he offers lift your glass and say ˙eeyi'a˙ meaning health what virtually all Greeks regard and value as the most important thing in life.

If you are unfortunate enough to be invited into aGreek home for a meal or for anything, and as luck would have it you just started on your 29th diet of the year, you're out of luck. You'll be lavished upon with several helpings of everything in the house. You will start with KALI OREKSI-bon apetit, and you won't be done till all is gone...and your diet too.You'll start eating when served, no need to wait till everybody else is, and you'll finish several hours later with the hostess looking on and asking if there is something else you would care for.

Car headlights are to communicate with other drivers, and so are car horns used anywhere from freely to abundantly although I haven't quite figured out yet what they all mean with the exception of anger and madness.

Questions such as "what do you do?"," how much money do you make?" and "how much did you pay for it?" are not at all indiscreet. Why on earth would you think they were? Well a Greek may ask you all that in one breath and think nothing of it. It is his way of expressing genuine interest and very few things are considered personal enough not to discuss.

The good nature of the Greeks manifests itself in another way. There is a wish for everything besides the normal things like birthdays, Christmas e.t.c. There is also name

Days the days the Saint"s or prophet's memory you were named after is celebrated. You again hear Hronia pola-many happy returns. This wish thing does not stop there. Oh No !!! It goes on and on.

KALO KALOKERI = Good Summer to you.

KALES DIAKOPES = Good vacation to you.

KALO H I MONA = Good winter to you.

KALO SAVATOKYRIAKO = Good weekend to you.

KALI VDOMADA = Good week to you-on Mondays only

KALO M I NA = Good month to you- 1st of the month
only,but sometimes 2nd ,3rd,4th e.t.c.
KALI OREKSI = Bon apetit-enjoy your food

KALI HONEPSI =Good ....Digestion to you

KALO TAX I D I =Good voyage- Bon voyage

KALOS EERTHATE =Welcome to our house

KALOS SAS VRIKAME =(response to above) Good to
have come and found you well.
KALI KSEKOURASI = Good rest to you.

KALO MATH I MA = Have a good lesson. E.T.C. E.T.C.

AND NOW USEFUL PHONE NUMBERS

POLICE
asti-no-mi'a   100

TOURIST POLICE   171

E.O.T.
Greek Tourist Organization   322-3111
                                         to-3119
also   322-2545
                        325-2267 and 322-8547
8 a.m.-2 p.m. and 2:30 p.m.-8 p.m.
Festivals   323-4467

CONSULATES

AUSTRALIA   644-7303
CANADA   723-9511
SOUTH AFRICA   692-2125
U.K.   723-6211
U.S.A.   721-2951
JAPAN   775-8101
GERMANY   369-4111

This is just enough for general information and emergencies.

AN EASY RECIPE

(this **is** a catch-all chapter after all, isn't it-**BONUS**)
FEWER THAN 24 HOURS TO PREPARE

KEFTETHES

INGREDIENTS
2 EGGS
1 CUP BREADCRUMBS
1 GRATED ONION
1 LEMON-JUICED
2 TSPS CHOPPED PARSLEY
2 TSPS CHOPPED MINT

SERVES 1-6
2 TSPS SALT
BLACK PEPPER
2.2 LBS GROUND BEEF
FLOUR
OLIVE OIL

PROCESS
1. BEAT EGGS-DEEP BOWL
2. MIX- IN EVERYTHING EXCEPT M EAT- FLOUR-OIL
3. LEAVE ALONE -15 MINUTES. WATCH SOAP OPERA
4. ADD M EAT AND MIX WELL WITH OWN HANDS
5. COVER AND PUT IN FRIG -1 HR. CONTINUE SOAP ON TV
6. SHAPE INTO GOLF BALLS FLATTENED
7. ROLL IN FLOUR
8. FRY IN HOT OIL-SHALLOW -3-4 MINS PER SIDE
9. TAKE OUT OF PAN AND DRY ON PAPER
10. EAT IF YOU DARE

* Keftedes go well with a Greek salad and fried potatoesand of course for the real afficionado what else but Retsina. * If you wish to serve them as a party appetizer shape them round and about the size of a walnut-regular before, small after frying.

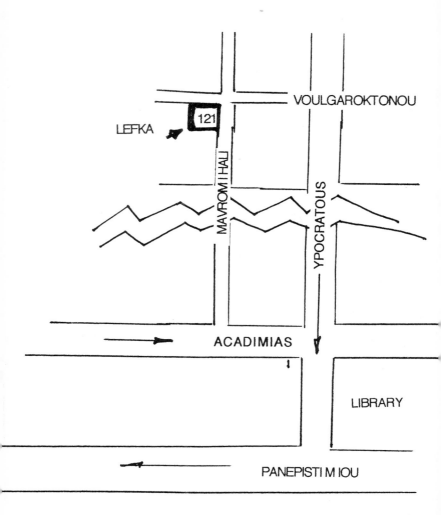

MAP TO KOUTOUKI 'H ΛΕΥΚΑ'-THE POPLAR

KOUTOUKIA LIST
(as promised earlier on)

Athens

MANOLIAS

PLATONOS 130
Acadimia Platonos

ZESTI GONIA

OLOFYTOU
Lambrini   222-0616

SPETSOPOULA

SPETSOPOULAS 3
Kipseli   823-2628

STAVROS

EUFORIONOS 13
Pangrati   701-9727

KOSTAS SIARKOS

VALAORITOU 15 *
Halandri   681-5166

* Retired Greek Opera House tenors frequent this tavern and often get in the mood.

KRITI

DIDIMOU & ALKIVIADOU*
                         881-7191

* Since 1907

DIGRESSION #2

I know I made a whole case about why I decided against making shopping suggestions. Since this is a catch-all section however, I'll make an exception. One and only. And it regards art and an artist whom I just met today, eventhough I had visited his shop several times in the past. And I have a soft spot for art, the real stuff that is. His name is John or Yiannis in Greek and he has a shop in Plaka, or at least in its outskirts. Its called SYNTHETON at 44a VOULIS St. John is a sculptor-ceramicist and I like his stuff. It's the real thing and it's good. You may or you may not like it as all art is a matter of personal taste as we all know. John's art has touched me because his small sculpture combines the beauty of the classics with that of the modern. A difficult thing to do. I've tried it. He uses materials from both and is both serious and whimsical, two more notions that are difficult to combine. His shapes are original and superbly executed. This is the type of memento I would gladly carry back with me. And it is very reasonably priced.

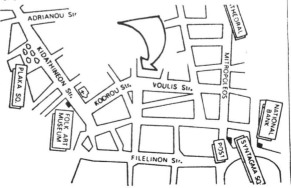

V I

TEST

QUALIFYING PRE-TEST
FOR *THE* TRIP

YES--NO

1- HAVE YOU EVER TRAVELLED MORE THAN
   100 MILES FROM HOME?   --------- -------

2- HAVE YOU EVER BEEN TO EXOTIC PLACES
   LIKE KOKOMO?   --------- ------

3- DO YOU FEEL SAFE AND COMFORTABLE
   RACING AN AUTOMOBILE WITH NO REGU-
   LATIONS WHATSOEVER?   --------- ------

4- HAVE YOU EVER HAD A SUBLIMINAL
   URGE TO JAY-WALK?   --------- ------

5- DO YOU ENJOY LOUD AND BOYSTEROUS
   PLACES?   --------- ------

6- HAVE YOU EVER JAY-WALKED?   --------- ------

7- CAN YOU ACT SURLY AND RUDELY?   --------- ------

8- DO YOU LIKE WAITING IN LINES LOOSE-
LY RESEMBLING A MOB?   ---------- ------

9- DO YOU RELISH THE THOUGHT OF FRIED
INTERNAL ANIMAL ORGANS FOR LUNCH?   ----------- -------

10- HOW ABOUT EXTERNAL ANIMAL PARTS
THEN?   --------- -------

11-DO YOU FEEL UNCOMFORTABLE WHEN
PEOPLE AROUND YOU SPEAK A FOREIGN
LANGUAGE?   --------- ---------

12- ARE YOU ILL AT EASE WHEN PEOPLE SPEAK
TO YOU IN ENGLISH THAT SOUNDS LIKE A
FOREIGN LANGUAGE?   ---------- ----------

13- DO YOU LIKE TALKING WITH YOUR HANDS?   ----------- -------

14-DO YOU LIKE TO USE OTHER PARTS OF
YOUR BODY TO COMMUNICATE?   ----------- --------

15- CAN YOU TRY TO UNDERSTANDTHE UNI-
VERSAL HAND -ARM WAVE ARGOT?   ----------- ------

16- ARE YOU TOLERANT OF OTHERS' MIS-
BEHAVIOR IF IT DOESN'T AFFECT OR
EFFECT YOU?   ----------- --------

16.5- HOW ABOUT JUST PLAIN GOOD OLD
BIZARRE ACTIONS?   ----------- -------

16.75-OR SOMEWHAT ECCENTRIC QUIRKS?   ------------- ------

17-ARE YOU SLIGHTLY TOLERANT OF OTHERS'
BEHAVIOR IF IT DOES EFFECT YOU? ---------- ---

18- CAN YOU DISREGARD YOUR VALUE SYSTEM
OR AT LEAST SUSPEND IT FOR A WHILE? ---------- ----

19- CAN YOU LET YOUR HAIR DOWN OR DO YOU
LIKE IT UP ALL THE TIME? ---------- ---

20-DO YOU NEED A HAIRCUT? ---------- -------

21- ARE YOU PATIENT OR AT LEAST DO YOU
THINK YOU ARE? ---------- ---

22- ARE YOU A PEOPLE WATCHER? ---------- --------

23- ARE YOU A PEOPLE WATCHER WITHOUT
NECESSARILY BEING ABLE TO TELL WHAT
THEY ARE DOING, OR WHETHER THAT WHICH
THEY ARE DOING IS A DIRECT OR EVEN AN
INDIRECT THREAT TO YOU?

---------- ----

24- MUST YOUR MORNING COFFEE TASTE LIKE
COFFEE? --------- -----------

25- COULD YOUR MORNING COFFEE HAVE
A CURIOUSLY UNDETERMINED BUT
SEDUCTIVE TASTE? ---------- ---------

26-DO YOU GET A KICK OUT OF RANDOMLY
BLOWING YOUR CAR HORN? ---------- ------

27- DO YOU GET A KICK WHEN OTHERS TOOT
   THEIR CAR HORNS WHIMSICALLY?   ------------   --------

28- DO YOU GET A THRILL OUT OF RISKING TO
   WALK ACROSS THE STREET OR EVEN ON THE
   SIDEWALK?   ----------   -------

29- DO YOU EVER GET AN UNTAMABLE
   STRONG IMPULSE TO WRING SOMEONES
   NECK?   ----------   -------

30- NOW ,REALLY LET ME ASK YOU.DO YOU
   LOVE YOUR MOTHER? AND DOES SHE LOVE
   YOU?   -----------   ---------

RESULTS

YESES   -------

NOS   -------

MAYBES   ------

SOLUTIONS: LOOK AT THE
OPPOSITE PAGE IF YOU DARE!

HOW TO RANK AND RATE YOUR CHANCES

1-5 YESES- STAY HOME, MAYBE EVEN MOVE TO A
FARMHOUSE IN ALABAMA

5-10 YESES- GO AS FAR AS MOBILE

10-15 DO NOT VENTURE OUTSIDE YOUR COUNTRY
AND DO AVOID BIG CITIES

15-20 YOU MAY START FOREIGN TRAVEL WITH
A QUICK VISIT TO EPCOT CENTER

20-25 GO TO ENGLAND OR AUSTRALIA FOR
A WEEK

26- GO TO ANY PART OF THE U.K. FOR MORE
THAN A WEEK

27- YOU MAY TRAVEL TO EUROPE AT WILL

28- YOU MAY TRAVEL TO ANY PARTS OF THE
WORLD, EVEN THE DANGEROUS ZONES

29- NOW YOU CAN GO TO GREECE FOR
A WEEK

30- **YOU MUST MOVE TO GREECE
IMMEDIATELLY**
(You just do not belong anywhere else)

VII

EPILOGUE

EPILOGUE
which could have been a prologue as well

The enormous expansion of the travel and tourist industries in the post-war years, and the relative ease and speed with which one can travel incredible distances, has turned the globe into a huge tourist mecca, with both good and evil repercussions. The statistics are mind boggling. 22 - 23 million people visit Orlando's Disney World in a year. Billions of air miles are travelled yearly by people going from one place to another with a fervor of overactive ants.

I'm all for it and all against it. I'd want every person on earth to see the Sistine Chapel, the Louvre, to experience the beauty of the Greek islands, the Grand Canyon, Iguazu Falls, to see and hear Rio De Janeiro, Paris, Tokyo, Sydney. I just don't want them to be there when I am there. I've been to the Disney Worlds of the world. No, thank you. Tis not for me.

I've also been to Great Resort Hotels where everything is provided for you. That's not for me either. I've been to cruises and travel tours of the "If its Tuesday, it must be Paris" variety. No, thanks. I am independent. Regardless how I travel, air, train, bus, car, camper or boat I like to be on my own. I prefer private means of transport, cars, campers and sailboats are fine. This way I can go where I want to, stop where and when I want to and start again when I decide to move on. I like the cities, but also the country, museums as well as out of the way little churches. The destination is only part of the fun. There are a whole lot of joys in the trip itself. I avoid busy places if I can. It is difficult to go to the British Museum any time of the year without being mobbed. This you cannot avoid. There are places though, and seasons where the mob scene can be avoided. Off-season is great for popular spots. The difficulty, for people like me, is to find spots in season that are not discovered and perhaps never will be, and to enjoy the tranquility, the slow pace, the real people, the good local food. I think there are others such as me (or should it be such as I?) For those of you then, unique and wonderful individuals, who could well be my friends, this little book was written.

I discover new peaceful places all the time, and I want to share them with you if you promise to leave them as you found them.

Greece is a magnificent land, and it is occupied (inhabited I should have said, but much of the time it appears that the Greeks are an occupational force in their own land if not prisoners of one another) by a marvellous if unpredictable and unique and contradictory people, unhampered by any known convention or conditioning. They have their very own.

Enjoy then the vistas, the smells, the tastes, the sounds of this land and if you're anything like me feel with al your senses.

Try not to think and not to judge, admittedly an impossible task for me. Just feel Greece. She is exhilarating.

ABOUT THE AUTHOR

Mr Elliott, as you may have gathered, is a unique sort of individual. Semi-educated at various universities in the US, he has graduated without and with honors from a couple of them, but will not admit to it. He has never been able to concentrate long enough on any one career in particular. His father urged him to become a nuclear physicist or at least a computer programmer in his early years, but gave up any hopes as the young lad quickly changed interests from kite flying to chocolate eating, to religion, scuba diving, sky diving, philosophy, hang gliding (but not aeronautics), and sailing, which he pursued with keen attention. As he was growing up in his mid-twenties he discovered Art and for a period of time he concentrated on painting, sculpture and pottery, save a few other areas such as economics, finance and teaching.

Still growing up in his thirties he discovered traveling, music, poetry and literature and rediscovered sailing. Throughout he continued eating enormous amounts of chocolate in every country he visited and has written an unpublished World Chocolate Guide which led him to the business world, opening and later selling several small Ishops. To satisfy his needs to live in an aesthetic environment, he converted an abandoned electrical substation into a four bedroom home to suit the needs of his family which included three young sons. He did the project himself, listening to no one in particular except to his, by then, exasperated wife at the time.

Moving right along and still growing up in his forties, he discovered sailing again and photography and writing for fun and profit. So far he has only been able to accomplish the fun part of it and to buy a few chocolate bars with the "profit" even though he has written and published 4 - 5 books and is on the planning stages of 3 - 4 more.

Well into his fifties now, and still growing up, he has taken up dancing, which he always sort of loved, and you'll find him virtually in every free public celebration where Brazilian sambas or Greek island dances are played, although he likes to tango every now and then, and to waltz if there is enough room.   He rediscovered philosophy and has read everything that Woody Allen and Lily Tomlin have written.

His three sons, fully grown up by now, as well as his father, in his nineties have all given up and when asked what Vernon is up to now, almost in unison they answer "Oh well, what can you do? Who knows? You know Vernon."

WHAT OTHERS SAY

Did you edit this ? Some of these sentences don't make any sense to me.

ANAST. MOSCHOPOULOS

Mr Elliott has mellowed considerably over the years. Lord knows he needed to.

AN UNFRIEND

NO, not again !!

HIS MOTHER

Why doesn't Vernon stick to sky diving ? -preferably without a parachute.

HIS BEST FRIEND

Vernon's niece (second cousin once removed in the U.S.) Eliana, is the only one with any writing talent in the family.

HIS UNCLE STAVROS

For the sake of propriety it has been decided not to quote newspaper and magazine critics.

BY THE SAME AUTHOR

1. GREEK : A FRACTURED LEXICON   VOLUME I
   Over 300 idioms,phrases,pejoratives and
   sounds, absolutely necessary to
   communicate in Greek or even to amuse
   yourself.

2. GREEK : A FRACTURED LEXICON   VOLUME II
   125 or so more of the above.

3. A VISITOR'S GUIDE TO MODERN GREEK BEHAVIOR
   AND HABITS
   A tongue-in-cheek approach to the culture
   shock.

4. A VISITOR'S GUIDE TO GREEK DRIVING ? AND
   OTHER OXYMORA AND PARADOXA
   1001 things a visitor needs to know, or just
   to laugh.

5. GREECE WITHOUT TEARS
   A guide for those who prefer the
   non-touristy approach to travel.

Mr Elliott has authored several other works which,
however, no publisher has dared as yet to accept.

ORDER FORM

PLEASE MAIL TO--
AT   --

GREEK- A FRACTURED LEXICON I $ 12.00   _____
GREEK- A FRACTURED LEXICON II   6.00   _____
GREEK BEHAVIOR & HABITS   6.00   _____
GREEK DRIVING   6.00   _____
GREECE WITHOUT TEARS   6.00   _____

POSTAGE & HANDLING $ 2.50 FIRST + $ .50 each additional

VISA-MC-AMEX-CHECK-M.OM.--

SPECIAL WHOLESALE PRICES AVAILABLE FOR FUND
RAISERS, BOOK STORES, TRAVEL AGENCIES E.T.C.

MAIL TO:
REGENT
4655 NORTH U.S. 41
NAPLES FLORIDA
33940   tel. 813-263-6622